SPOT THE MISTAKE

A Chapter Two book
created by Amanda Wood and Mike Jolley

Quarto is the authority on a wide range of topics.

Quarto educates, entertains and enriches the lives of our readers—enthusiasts and lovers of hands-on living.

www.quartoknows.com

First published in Great Britain in 2017 by Wide Eyed Editions,
an imprint of Aurum Press, 74–77 White Lion Street, London N1 9PF
QuartoKnows.com
Visit our blogs at QuartoKnows.com

Illustrations copyright © Frances Castle 2017
Text copyright © Chapter Two 2017

A catalogue record for this book is available from the British Library.

ISBN 978-1-84780-963-6

The illustrations were created digitally
Set in Bellota Regular

Text by Amanda Wood
Design by Mike Jolley
Edited by Eryl Nash
Published by Rachel Williams

Printed in China

SPOT THE MISTAKE

AMANDA WOOD & MIKE JOLLEY

LANDS OF LONG AGO

ILLUSTRATED BY FRANCES CASTLE

WIDE EYED EDITIONS

1 SURVIVING IN THE STONE AGE
2 LAND OF THE PHARAOHS
3 AN OUTING TO THE ACROPOLIS
4 THE EMPEROR'S PALACE
5 LIFE IN ANCIENT ROME

It's going to be such fun to dress up in all these historical costumes!

WHAT'S WRONG WITH THIS BOOK?

How much do you think you know about history? Did you know that the ancient Romans had a huge army? Or that the Vikings sailed about in longboats? If the answer is yes, then it's time to pit your wits against the puzzles in this book.

But first, a word of warning – history just got all mixed up!

On the following pages, you'll find 10 scenes of life from long ago – from Stone Age farmers to jousting knights,

6
AT THE TEMPLE
OF THE SUN

7
SAILING WITH
THE VIKINGS

8
JOUSTING WITH
THE KNIGHTS

9
THE EMPEROR'S
PARADE

10
PIRATES
AHOY!

and Egyptian pharaohs to plundering pirates. Look closely and you'll soon see that not all is as it should be. Each picture contains 20 things that shouldn't be there – a Mayan wearing a wristwatch, a Roman soldier wearing jeans, a Greek vase in ancient China... Pretty obvious, right? But some things might be a little harder to spot. So, we've enlisted the help of two young history detectives to give you a helping hand along the way. Plus, if you get really stuck, just turn the page to find all the answers, as well as some really interesting facts about what these ancient guys actually *did* have back in the day.

HAPPY HUNTING!

1

NEOLITHIC STONE AGE

Northern Europe

Around 4000 – 2400 BC

2

New Kingdom
ANCIENT EGYPT

Egypt

Around 1550 – 1070 BC

3

ANCIENT GREECE

Greece

Around 776 – 146 BC

4

Han Dynasty
ANCIENT CHINA

China

Around 206 BC – AD 220

5

ANCIENT ROME

Italy

Around 27 BC – AD 476

WHO, WHERE, WHEN?

Humans have come a long way since our ancestors first walked on Earth 2.5 million years ago. It took us a long while to get civilised – to wear clothes, grow our own food and start building things – but once we started, our progress was amazingly quick. If the whole of our planet's history was condensed into just one year, then the first civilisations would only appear just before midnight on the very last day of December! It's hard to get your head around it, especially as things didn't always happen at the same time everywhere in the world.

Around 250 BC – AD 900

Around AD 793 – 1066

12th – 15th centuries

16th century

17th and 18th centuries

6

Classic period
MAYANS
Central America

7

VIKINGS
Scandinavia

8

MEDIEVAL KNIGHTS
Europe

9

MUGHALS
India

10

PIRATES
Caribbean

The first farmers started to grow crops around the Mediterranean in about 9000 BC, but the idea didn't reach Northern Europe for another 4,500 years – that's a long time to wait for a bowl of porridge... Anyway, above you can see a timeline that shows you the who, where and when of all the people you're about to meet in the following pages.

I've always wanted to be a knight!

SURVIVING IN THE STONE AGE

Around 12,000 years ago, there was a big change to the way human beings lived in Northern Europe. Up until this time, in the Early Stone Age, humans had moved from place to place, hunting and gathering food as they went. But towards the Middle Stone Age, they got fed up with all that walking about and decided to stay in one place. By around 4000 BC, in a period known as the Neolithic, or Late Stone Age, they were growing crops, keeping animals and building permanent homes. This was the start of community living!

But can you spot the 20 things you wouldn't have seen in the Stone Age?

There are easier ways of spray painting, you know!

1. House. Staying in one place meant that people could build more permanent shelters to live in, but they wouldn't have been able to build a brick house like this one. Instead, they made their homes from timber, with walls of 'wattle' (woven hazel rods) smeared with 'daub' (a plaster-like substance made from clay, straw and cow dung). A thatched roof topped it all off.

2. Chickens. Stone Age farmers would have kept the ancestors of our modern day cattle, sheep and goats. They would also have bred pigs from the wild boar that lived in the woods of Neolithic Britain, but they wouldn't have had chickens. These did not become common in Britain until the Romans made them popular as a source of food.

3. Birthday cake. We don't really know if Stone Age people celebrated their birthdays, but they certainly wouldn't have done it with birthday cake. Although they farmed the first seed grains, like wheat, oats and barley and had learned to grind them into flour, they could only make simple flatbreads rather than elaborate cakes (and they didn't have any candles to go on the top, either).

4. Kilt. Early humans cleaned, prepared and made clothes out of animal skins to protect themselves and keep warm. By the Late Stone Age they had also learned to spin plant fibres into simple cloth. They may even have died it different colours but they would not have been able to make this colourful kilt.

5. Jam jar. Although it's possible that Stone Age people made a kind of jam out of cooked berries, they didn't have handy glass jars to keep it in. Humans had instead been making pots out of stone or wood for thousands of years, and in the Neolithic period they discovered how to make simple bowls and pots out of clay – heated up in an open fire to make the first pottery.

6. Sweetcorn is a type of maize that was not known outside of the Americas until it was given to European settlers in the 18th century. Stone Age cooks weren't short on ingredients, though – they ate lots of other plants such as wild onions, the bulbs of lilies (roasted), apples, nuts, seeds, berries and all sorts of leafy green plants (such as nettles and sea beet). And then there was all the meat, fish, birds' eggs and honey. Yum!

7. Saucepan. Cooking must have been tricky without metal pots and pans but those Stone Age chefs had other tricks up their sleeves. They would roast or boil meat in simple pots or lay it over hot stones to cook.

8. Ladder. Stonehenge in Dorset is probably the most famous prehistoric monument in the world. It was constructed over many hundreds of years, starting around 5,000 years ago, but its builders didn't have ladders to help them with its construction. We don't know for sure how it was made, but scientists think the huge stones were hauled into place using earth ramps and ropes made from plant fibres and tree bark.

9. Easter Island statue. Although they made stone circles and other enormous stone monuments, Stone Age people didn't carve them into human shapes. This stone head comes from an island in the Pacific Ocean and was carved by ancient Polynesians many thousands of years after Stonehenge was created.

10. Dinosaurs were not around by the time Stone Age man appeared – they had died out about 65 million years before. But the hunters of the day still hunted down other prehistoric creatures, such as mammoths and woolly rhinos, as well as deer, bears and wolves.

11. Net. Stone Age hunters had to rely on simple hand axes made from sharpened flint and flint arrow heads fastened onto wooden throwing spears to help them catch their food, rather than using throwing nets. To catch really big animals (like mammoths, which were REALLY enormous), they drove them into swamps or over the edges of cliffs.

12. Neanderthal man. The earliest human-like animals, our ancestors, evolved from apes many millions of years ago. By the Late Stone Age all other species, including this Neanderthal man, had died out, leaving only *Homo sapiens* (us)! With our bigger brains we had soon learned to make the most of things – inventing language, making the first tools and living together in small communities.

20 things you wouldn't have found in the Stone Age

13. Sword. In the Stone Age, metal had yet to be discovered (that's why it was called the Stone Age) so they wouldn't have had any handy iron swords to help them fight off woolly mammoths.

14. Zebra skin. No Stone Age man would have been seen draped in a zebra skin. Leather and furs made from deer, bear or wolf skins were the fashions of the day, prepared by scraping the skins with specially sharpened flints.

15. Gravestone. Neolithic people didn't bury their dead in graves with headstones like this. Instead, they made collective tombs called 'long barrows', where the dead could be laid out and even visited by their relatives. They would have had many chambers and would have been constructed of stone or wood and covered in earth.

16. Painting of a tiger. Lots of cave paintings made in the Stone Age have been discovered all over the world but those in Northern Europe would not have featured tigers. One famous discovery in a cave in Lascaux, France, included thousands of painted figures – of deer, bulls, horses and bears, as well as humans.

17. Aerosol can. Although they didn't have aerosol paints, Stone Age artists did invent a primitive form of airbrushing by blowing paint through a hollowed-out bone to create images. Usually the paint, made from natural pigments mixed with water or animal fat, was swabbed or blotted on to the surface, or drawn on with charcoal.

18. Graffiti. Written language had not been invented in the Stone Age so you would not have found graffiti like this on the walls of a Stone Age cave.

19. Bangles. Men were not known to wear metal bangles but they did string shells together to make necklaces.

20. Calendar. Stone Age people wouldn't have had a printed wall calendar but it is possible that Stonehenge itself worked as a kind of giant stone calendar – measuring out the seasons and the passage of the Sun and Moon through the sky.

SURVIVING IN THE STONE AGE

The start of farming – when humans learned how to produce, rather than hunt down, their food – was one of the biggest changes in human history. It happened at different times in different places around the world and by 4500 BC had reached the part of Northern Europe that we now call Britain. The switch to farming led to all sorts of other changes to the way humans lived in the Late Stone Age – not just how they got their food. They built huge stone monuments, began living in small communities of simple houses and learned to make pottery and weave cloth.

LAND OF THE PHARAOHS

The ancient Egyptians lived a long, long time ago – about 5,000 years ago in fact. But don't think that means they were cavemen living in, well, *caves* and wearing the skin of dead animals. In reality, they were very sophisticated people. They built the first large stone buildings, invented one of the earliest forms of writing and were pretty good at preserving dead bodies. Thanks to that, we know a lot about them.

Test your knowledge by seeing if you can spot 20 things in the picture that the Egyptians didn't have.

20 things? That's going to be difficult...

EMBALMING FLUID

LAND OF THE PHARAOHS

The great kingdom of ancient Egypt sprang up along the borders of the River Nile, surrounded by miles and miles of desert. It was here that the Egyptians built their immense pyramids and secret tombs to hold the mummies of their dead; where they farmed the fertile land along the banks of the river and where the pharaohs ruled their people for more than 3,000 years – from around 3100 BC. The ancient Egyptians were one of the most advanced civilisations of their time.

I didn't spot ALL the mistakes, and I was there!

1. **Modern clothing.** The ancient Egyptians fashioned many beautiful objects out of solid gold – like statues of their gods and pharaohs – but not one of this girl wearing modern dress.

2. **Vampire.** Because they believed their dead would join the gods in the afterlife, the ancient Egyptians took great care of dead bodies. They preserved them through a process called 'mummification', but they did not bury them in this type of wooden coffin – nor did they believe in vampires!

3. **Embalming fluid.** The mummification process involved drying out the body using a special salt called 'natron' and then wrapping it in layer-upon-layer of bandages. It was then placed in a special type of coffin called a 'sarcophagus'. Often there would be two or three sarcophagi, packed one inside the other, made of solid gold or painted wood. However, the priests responsible for making mummies didn't have the benefit of today's embalming fluid to help them.

4. **Teddy bear jar.** Another part of mummification involved the removal of the dead person's internal organs (yuk)! These were kept in special containers called 'canopic jars' and housed in a shrine. The jars often had lids in the shape of the different gods; they wouldn't have had one in the shape of a teddy!

5/6. **Power drill/ cement mixer.** The great pyramids of ancient Egypt were the world's first great buildings. Made as tombs for the pharaohs, they were built of enormous rock blocks using only the simplest of tools. Thousands of labourers would have toiled away for years to create them, without the help of modern equipment like this.

7. **Fir tree.** The Land of the Pharaohs was a pretty hot place, surrounded by dry, sandy deserts. Date palms and other desert plants would have been common – but not this type of tree, which comes from a much colder climate.

8. **Cars** like this would not have been invented for thousands of years, but the ancient Egyptians did have chariots. Chariot-racing was a popular sport with the pharaohs and they were also used for hunting, in battle and to carry the pharaoh in state processions. The great King Tutankhamun even had several chariots buried with him in his pyramid!

9. Church. As well as pyramids, the ancient Egyptians built great temples to worship their gods, but they didn't build churches like the one shown here.

10. Dragon god. Although they worshipped a large number of gods, often in the form of animals, they would not have had a god in the

12. Vicar. Priests were an important part of daily life in the pharaoh's court. They were responsible for many important rituals to ensure the good fortune of the kingdom, but they would not have worn clothing like this Christian vicar. Instead, they wore simple linen tunics and

14. Fez. Most clothing in Egypt at this time was made of linen, woven from the fibres of the flax plant, or from animal hide. Because it was so hot, the clothing was very light and slaves often went completely naked. Although the nobles may have worn elaborate wigs to

including wheat and barley. They also grew many vegetables and fruits, including figs, melons, pomegranates and grapes, but not carrots – which would not be grown as a crop for thousands of years.

17. Tractor. Egyptian farmers used a lightweight plough pulled by oxen to till their soil, not a modern machine like this.

18. Hosepipe. The waters of the Nile were very important in helping the Egyptians grow their crops. Annual flooding helped to keep the soil fertile and farmers built an enormous network of ditches and dams to funnel river water to their crops. They also invented an incredibly simple tool called a 'shadoof', to help lift water from the river onto the land. But they did not have hosepipes (or taps, for that matter).

19. Canoe. The Nile was the main highway of Egypt. Wooden boats called 'feluccas' carried passengers and cargo up and down the river, transporting everything from crops to the heavy stones needed for pyramid building. The Egyptians were among the first people to attach sails to their boats, which helped them travel faster and gave them better control. The Nile would have been filled with all sorts of water craft, from simple row boats made of papyrus to trading feluccas and fishing boats – even the pharaoh's boat covered with gold and fancy carvings – but you would not have seen this Native American canoe.

20 things to learn about ancient Egypt

shape of this dragon – which comes from ancient China.

11. Book. The Egyptians didn't have books (and certainly wouldn't have heard of Red Riding Hood)! But they were one of the first people to invent a system of writing. They used pictures called 'hieroglyphics' instead of words, with each symbol representing a sound, a word or an action. Instead of paper, they used flattened sheets or scrolls made from papyrus – a type of reed.

perhaps a robe made from the pelt of a leopard if they were very important – like the one worn by the person standing to his left.

13. Electric paddle fans weren't invented when the ancient Egyptians were around. Instead, one of the court servants would have had a full-time job as a fan bearer to the pharaoh. Made of gilded wood and ostrich feathers, these fans were used to create a cooling breeze but more elaborate versions were also used in state processions as a symbol of the pharaoh's divine power.

show their status, this slave would not have been allowed to wear anything on his head and certainly not a fez – a style of hat common in North Africa in the 1800s.

15. Bulldog. The pharaoh might have been fond of animals but he wouldn't have had a pet bulldog – a breed of dog developed solely in England. Instead, he might have kept a pet baboon, admired for its intelligence and also associated with Thoth, the Egyptian god of writing and wisdom.

16. Carrots. The Egyptians grew many crops,

20. Kangaroos. The Egyptians were some of the first people to regard hunting as a sport as well as a means to find food. Large areas around the Nile were preserved for hunting and fishing. Gazelle, antelope, hares and even hippos and crocodiles were hunted down using nets, spears and chariots and then eaten. Kangaroos, however, were not on the menu.

AN OUTING TO THE ACROPOLIS

Over 2,500 years ago, one of the world's greatest civilisations grew in mainland Greece. For hundreds of years, the ancient Greeks had a huge influence on life in the Western world. They invented lots of groovy things – from poetry to the Olympic games, theatres, libraries and coins with writing – even the system of politics we know as democracy. They were expert architects and built elaborate temples in honour of their gods and goddesses. Here you can see a typical day inside the Acropolis – a massive fortified citadel with the Parthenon temple at its centre. But can you spot 20 things that shouldn't be there?

1. **Shorts.** The Greeks invented the Olympic Games and held the first one in 776 BC, in honour of the god Zeus. Only men were allowed to take part and they all had to perform naked – no clothing was allowed, even these natty shorts!

2. **Torch.** Today's Olympic Games do involve a torch but not one that needs a battery. Instead, the modern Olympic torch is lit from a fire started at the site of the original Olympics, and then carried all the way to the city that is hosting the games. The Greeks kept a fire burning throughout the celebration of the ancient Olympics, too. Can you find it somewhere in the picture?

3. **Tennis.** Many different sports were performed at the Olympics – including running, long jump, javelin, discus, hockey and boxing, but definitely not tennis.

4. **Violin.** There were lots of different Greek gods (you can see some in the panel opposite) and the Greeks believed that the important ones lived in a cloud palace on top of Mount Olympus, the highest mountain in Greece. Each god controlled a different aspect of life and had special symbols associated with them. Here, you can see Apollo, god of music and medicine. He is usually shown with a lyre (a kind of harp) or a lute but definitely not this violin.

5. **Playbill for _Romeo and Juliet_.** Ancient Greece was full of great writers. Sophocles, for example, was one of the great Greek playwrights and his works are still performed today. However, he didn't write _Romeo and Juliet_ (that was the creation of another fellow called William Shakespeare, who lived in the 16th century) and even if he had, he wouldn't have had a printed playbill to advertise it!

6. **Microphone.** The Greeks were considered to be masters at the art of public speaking, or oration, but they would not have had a microphone to help themselves be heard. Being able to make speeches or win debates was considered an important skill, particularly as

Greece was a 'democracy' – a new form of government developed by the Athenians that meant people had a say in how they were governed. The great philosophers (thinkers) of the day would often be great orators, too, making long speeches and discussing everything from the nature of love to the meaning of life.

8. **Cameras** like this were not invented until the early 20th century. But the ancient Greeks did take the first step towards their development when Aristotle noticed how light passing through a small hole into a darkened room produced an image of the view outside on the opposite wall, but upside down. This so-called 'camera obscura' eventually led to the cameras we know today. Happy snapping!

things down using a wax tablet (a wooden board covered in a layer of wax) and a pointed instrument called a 'stylus'. In Athens, only boys had lessons at school (lucky them). Girls stayed at home and were taught to read and write by their mothers.

11. **English lettering.** The ancient Greeks had an alphabet a bit like ours but lots of the letters looked quite different, so you would not have seen a rhyme like this. Lots of English words

What's wrong in ancient Greece?

7. **Telegraph poles.** The ancient Greeks did not have telephones so they wouldn't have had telegraph poles, either. If they needed to get an urgent message to someone, they would have sent a runner to deliver it by hand. One important message delivered in this way gave its name to our modern day 'marathon' race. To deliver the news of the defeat of the Persians by Athenian troops in the Battle of Marathon, a messenger ran over 26 miles from Marathon to Athens, but after announcing the victory he promptly dropped down dead!

9. **Prams** (or 'perambulators', to give them their full name) were not invented until the 18th century in Britain. In ancient Greece, children would have been carried by their parents, or by the family's slaves, until they were old enough to walk themselves.

10. **Chalkboard.** Although the Greeks were big believers in education, their teachers would not have used chalkboards to teach lessons. Instead, subjects were read out loud and students had to memorise everything. They also wrote

come from Greek words, though, so you've probably spoken in Greek without even knowing it! The word 'alphabet', for example, is a Greek word, made from alpha (meaning 'a') and beta (meaning 'b').

12. **Lighting rig.** The theatre was an important part of life in ancient Greece but shows would not have been performed on a stage with a lighting rig like this. Instead the stage would have been semi-circular and surrounded by rows of raised seats to create what we call an 'amphitheatre'.

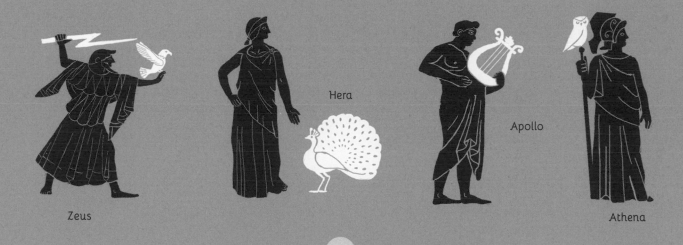

Zeus

Hera

Apollo

Athena

13. Jester. There were two main types of Greek play – tragedies (often about the past) and comedies (about everyday life). The plays often featured gods as some of the characters but would never have included this jester, even though he might have been pretty amusing!

14. Medieval castle. You wouldn't have found this typical English castle inside the Acropolis. The most impressive building there was the Parthenon – a large, elaborate temple. It was made of marble and decorated with friezes and statues painted in bright colours.

15. Statue of Henry VIII. The Greeks liked to have lots of statues about the place but they wouldn't have had one of Henry VIII – he wasn't even born until over a thousand years later! Often, the statues would be of one of the many Greek gods. People would pray to them and make sacrifices in the hope of getting everything from a good harvest to a pretty daughter.

16. Toucan. This statue shows the goddess Athena. She was the daughter of Zeus, king of the gods, and was the god that protected Athens (hence its name). The Parthenon was built in her honour. She was the goddess of wisdom and war and, like all the gods, she had special symbols associated with her, including a spear and an owl – but never this toucan from the rainforests of Brazil.

17. Rucksacks would not have been used for carrying things around in ancient Greece. Though they did make woven baskets, they also used pottery containers, called 'amphora', to transport all sorts of things – from wine and water to grain and olives – often by carrying them on their heads. See if you can find someone carrying an amphora in the picture...

18. Chinese lettering would not have been carved into the base of Athena's statue. Instead, it would have had an inscription written in ancient Greek or a frieze carved into the marble.

19. Poodle. This painting shows another Greek god - Hades, ruler of the underworld. He is usually depicted carrying his chief weapon, a two-pronged fork, and his three-headed dog Cerberus, rather than this much less savage poodle!

20. Fishing rod. Another chief god of Athens was Poseidon, god of the sea. He was often shown with his three-pronged trident and a dolphin, but never with a fishing rod (even though it might have come in useful).

3

AN OUTING TO THE ACROPOLIS

Ancient Greece is often called 'the birthplace of Western civilisation', and their way of life was admired and copied by lots of other people of the time. But even though they controlled a great empire and invented a whole bunch of useful stuff, it didn't stop them being defeated by the Romans in 146 BC. After that, the great Greek civilisation became part of the Roman Empire.

Luckily, we know quite a bit about what went on in ancient Greece from the artwork that they left behind, especially the many examples of painted pottery that have survived. These vases and pots, often painted with black figures on an orange-red background, show us everything from Olympic athletes, gods and goddesses to daily life. You can see some illustrations like this in the borders of the picture, but remember – not everything is quite correct!

Poseidon

Hermes

Aphrodite

Hades

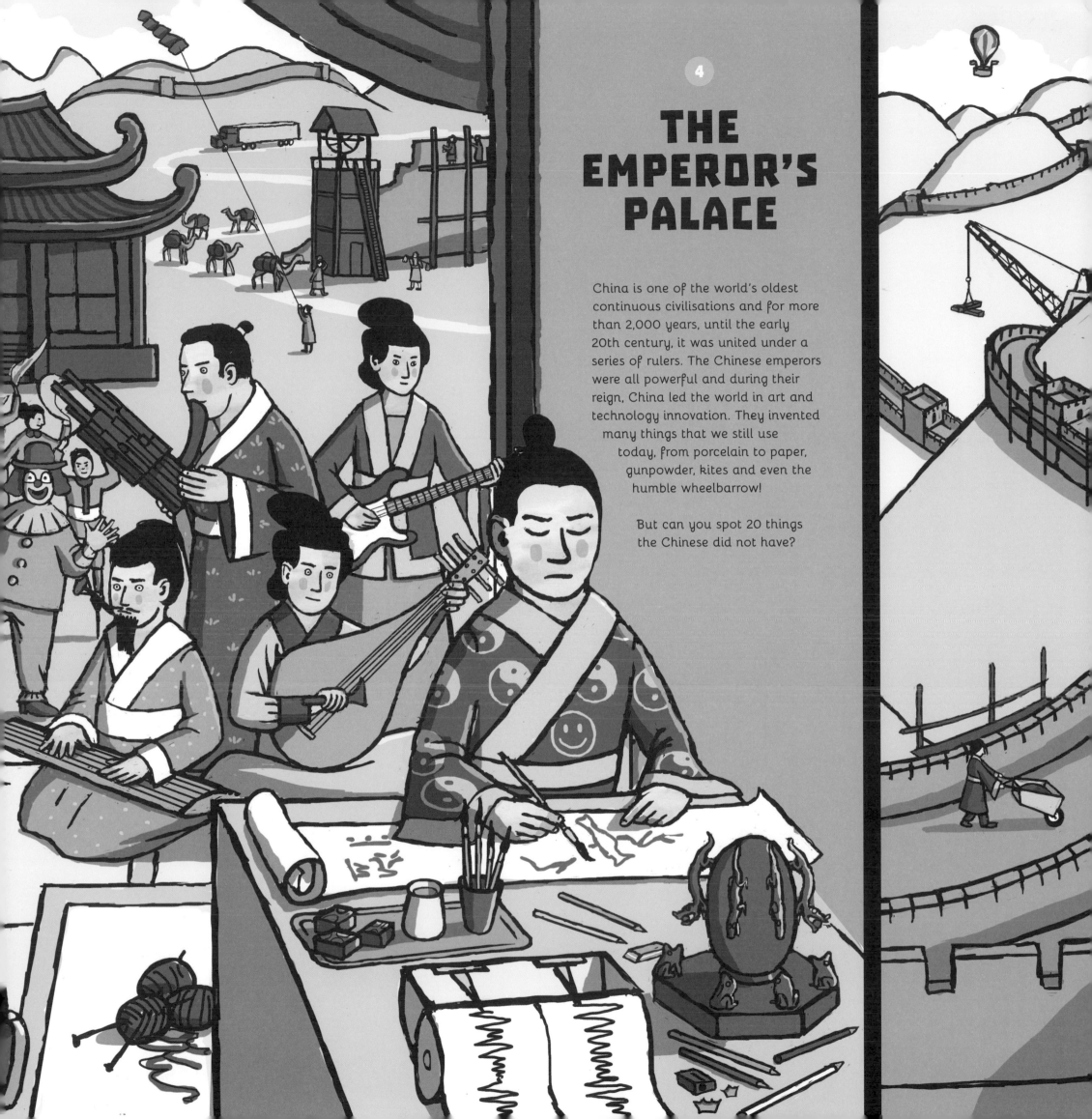

THE EMPEROR'S PALACE

China is one of the world's oldest continuous civilisations and for more than 2,000 years, until the early 20th century, it was united under a series of rulers. The Chinese emperors were all powerful and during their reign, China led the world in art and technology innovation. They invented many things that we still use today, from porcelain to paper, gunpowder, kites and even the humble wheelbarrow!

But can you spot 20 things the Chinese did not have?

THE EMPEROR'S PALACE

Many Chinese people think of the Han period as the true beginning of China. It was a time of exciting change and lots of advancements in technology and trade: Chinese merchants carried silk and other goods across central Asia to trade with countries along a route that became known as the Silk Road; skilled craftsmen learned how to make beautiful objects out of bronze porcelain (china!), and scientists of the time even invented an object for predicting earthquakes.

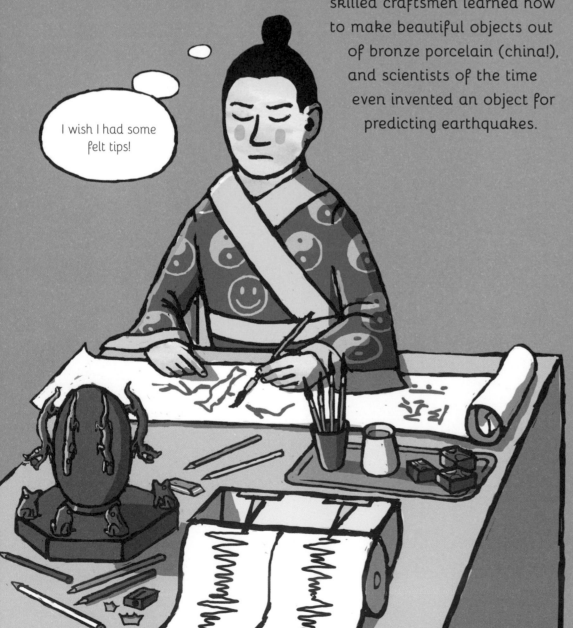

I wish I had some felt tips!

1. Giraffe statue. In around 100 BC, Chinese iron-workers invented the blast furnace. This enabled them to make a much wider range of better quality objects out of iron and bronze, such as the 2,000 year-old bronze horse you can see in the panel on the left. However, they would not have made this golden statue of a giraffe from Africa.

2. Greek vase. During the Han dynasty, the Chinese invented porcelain (which is why it's often called 'china'), making glazed vases, jars and models of everything from animals to buildings, many of which have been discovered in the graves of their owners. During an earlier dynasty, the first emperor of China, Qin Shi Huangdi, was buried in a tomb containing thousands of life-size models of his army, all made out of terracotta (an early form of pottery). But you would not have found this Greek vase among them.

3. Silver fork. The ancient Chinese would not have used forks to eat their food. Instead they relied on chopsticks. The first chopsticks were probably used for cooking or serving food but later began to be used as eating utensils.

4. Calculator. The ancient Chinese did not use a calculator to do their sums. Instead they used an abacus, or 'suanpan', consisting of metal rods strung with beads and held in a wooden frame. The abacus had been around for thousands of years and used by lots of different civilisations, such as the ancient Egyptians and the Romans, but the Chinese version could be used to do more complicated calculations.

5. Smiley face. Did you spot the smiley face among the 'yin' and 'yang' symbols in the border of the picture? Traditional Chinese beliefs are based on the idea that everything and everyone is made up of yin (darkness) and yang (lightness) and that health and happiness only come when these are in balance.

6. Fresco of the Madonna and Child. The ancient Chinese would not have followed the Christian religion or had frescoes like this on their wall. Instead, they worshipped their ancestors or followed a system of beliefs called Taoism. Buddhism also became common in China during the Han dynasty, having been brought from India by travellers along the Silk Road. Can you see a statue of the Buddha in the panel?

7. Newspaper. The Han dynasty had used silk as

a writing material before they invented paper. Although they went on to invent woodblock printing, they never made newspapers.

8. Blonde, curly hair would have been virtually unknown in ancient China, where most people had dark, straight hair. Most people wore their hair long – men often tied theirs into a knot on top of their head; women coiled it up and decorated it with hairpins, but they were only allowed to do this after they were married.

that having tiny feet was an essential part of feminine beauty, so young girls from rich families had their feet tightly bound to prevent them from growing. They wore tight fitting, beautifully embroidered shoes with thick heels or platforms so that they could only walk with tiny steps.

13. Balls of wool would not have been used to knit clothes in China. Instead, one of the most important and valuable raw materials was silk, woven from fibres taken from the cocoons of silkworms. Silk-making began in China over 5,000 years ago and it became such an

not invented until the 20th century. Instead, Han dynasty artists painted on silk or paper, using brush pens made of animal hair and ink made from pine soot and animal glue. The Chinese valued calligraphy (handwritten lettering) and painting as the purest forms of art.

16. Electric guitars wouldn't have formed part of the emperor's entertainments. Instead, his musicians might have played a type of lute called a 'pipa', a type of mouth organ called a 'sheng' or a stringed instrument called a 'qin zither'. Can you find all three in the picture?

Did you spot 20 Chinese mistakes?

17. Road trucks would not have been used to carry goods along the trading routes of ancient China. Camel trains (called 'caravans'), horses and sometimes even yak or oxen would have been loaded up with precious cargo, or it would have been carried on foot by traders and their servants.

18. Hot air balloon. Although you might have seen a colourful kite flying in the sky over ancient China, you would not have seen a hot air balloon – since they weren't invented until the 18th century. Kites, however, have been around in China since around 500 BC, firstly for military use and then for entertainment. They were made from silk or paper stretched over a bamboo frame.

19. Crane. One of the most important, and impressive, constructions of ancient China is the Great Wall, started by the first emperor around 220 BC. The longest structure ever created by humans, it winds for more than 21,000 kilometres across northern China and was built to keep out invaders. No cranes would have been available to help in its construction – peasants and soldiers would have laboured for many years to build it, using simple tools and scaffolding made of bamboo.

20. Metal wheelbarrows would not have been around in ancient China but the people of the Han dynasty did invent the first wooden wheelbarrow. It had a single central wheel and was known as a 'wooden ox'. Can you see one in the background of the picture?

9. Suit and tie. Clothing in ancient China was a symbol of status and would not have included the wearing of suits and ties. Poor people wore clothing made of hemp – a type of plant – woven into loose fitting trousers and shirts. Rich people wore clothing made of silk, often beautifully embroidered, and both men and women usually wore long robes called 'kimonos'.

10. High-heeled shoes like this were not seen in ancient China, though both noble men and women sometimes wore shoes with wooden platform soles. The Chinese also believed

11. Clocks like this would not have been found on the wall of pagodas in ancient China. However, the Chinese did invent some of the world's first astronomical clocks, powered by the energy of falling water.

12. Circus clown. Throughout the year in ancient China, there were festivals, including dancing, music and acrobatics, but you would not have seen this clown among the entertainers. Stilt walkers were a common sight, though – performing elaborate dances while standing on wooden stilts strapped to their feet.

important part of their culture and economy that details of its production were kept secret for over 2,000 years. The Chinese used it to make kimonos, to make wall hangings and, before they invented paper, as a writing material.

14. Seismometer. Although the Chinese would not have had this modern seismometer, they did invent the world's first earthquake detector – you can see it next to the seismometer on the table. Even the slightest tremor would cause the balls held in the dragons' mouths to drop into the waiting mouths of the frogs below.

15. Coloured pencils were not part of an artist's materials in ancient China – they were

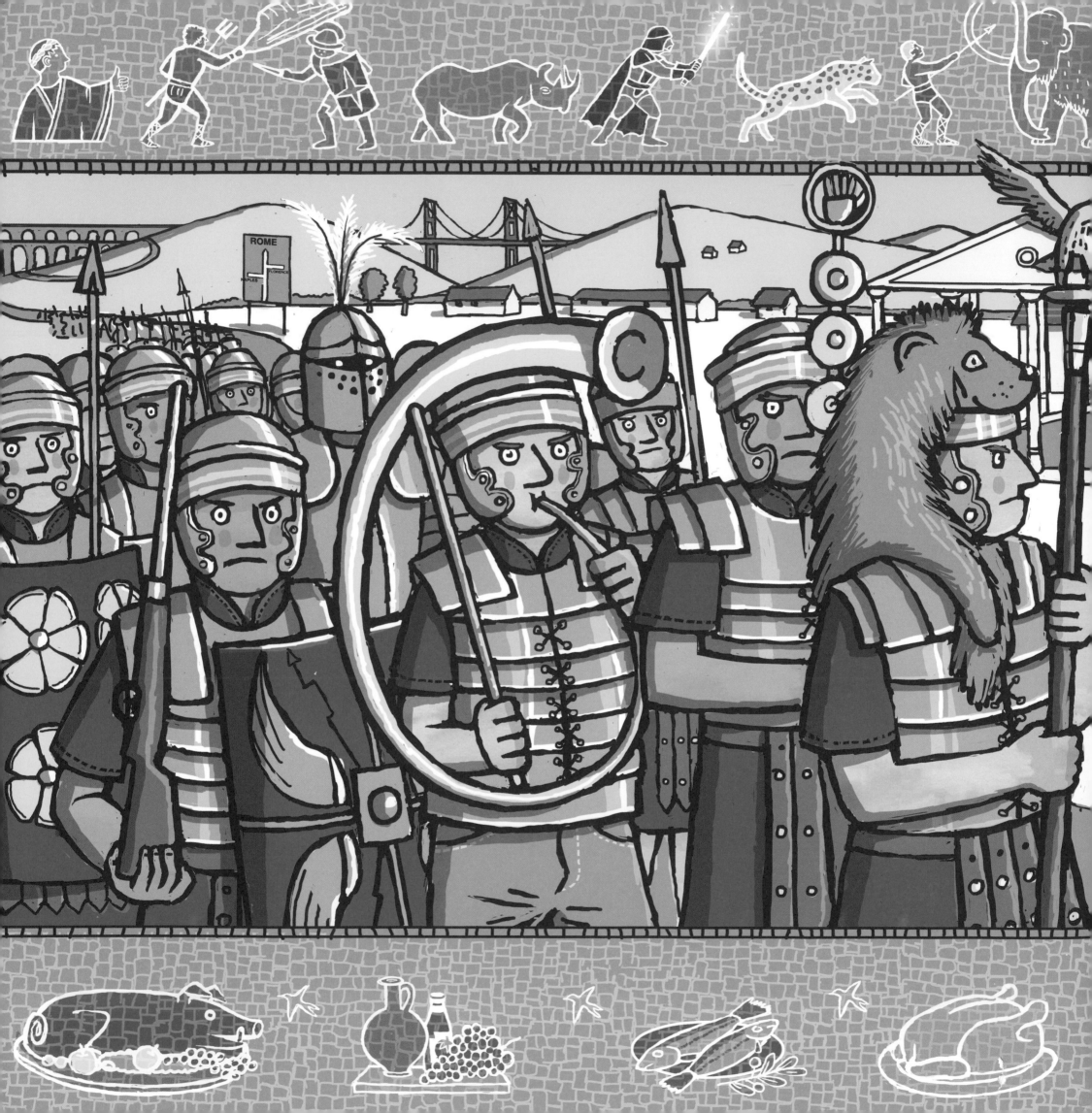

LIFE IN ANCIENT ROME

Although it began as a small village in central Italy, the city of Rome eventually ruled over one of the largest and most prosperous empires of all time. This had a lot to do with its army – a highly trained and well-equipped bunch of soldiers who were famous for their discipline and clever battle tactics. The ancient Romans were full of good ideas – they built huge networks of roads across their empire, were astonishing engineers and staged elaborate shows, where brave gladiators fought wild beasts for the entertainment of the public. Although they could be cruel, especially to their enemies, they spread wealth and stability across their great empire.

But can you spot 20 things that you would not have seen in Rome around 2,000 years ago?

1. Suspension bridge. The Romans were brilliant architects, especially if there was a practical problem that needed solving. They were great at building bridges, including a special type of bridge called an 'aqueduct', which they used to bring water from rivers in the countryside into the cities. The aqueducts were usually made of many arches (stone arches were just one of the many things those clever Romans invented) and you can still see them all over Europe today. But although they were good at building, the Romans hadn't yet mastered the art of building modern bridges such as this one – they weren't invented until the early 1800s.

2. Motorway sign. The Romans basically invented concrete and they used it to build a huge network of long, straight roads all across the empire. They even had road signs carved out of stone to tell you how far it was to the next city – but they would not have had a sign like this one.

3. Medieval knight. Without their army, the Romans wouldn't have had their empire. The best-trained soldiers were foot soldiers called 'legionaries'. They were organised into around 30 highly disciplined units called 'legions', which each contained between 4,000 and 6,000 soldiers. They were some of the first soldiers to have metal armour, which consisted of simple iron plates held together with leather ties – not nearly as elaborate (or as heavy) as the full suit of armour worn by this knight.

4. Jeans. Underneath their armour, soldiers wore short, woollen tunics, sometimes with a skirt made of leather strips studded with metal, but they didn't wear denim jeans (even though they might have been a lot more comfortable).

5. Rifle. Every legionary had a javelin (throwing spear), a short sword and a dagger as their main weapons for combat. They would not have carried a rifle into battle since no one had invented them at the time.

6. Daisy design. Roman soldiers carried big,

rectangular shields that they could form into a wall to protect themselves when marching shoulder-to-shoulder into battle. The shield would often carry the emblem of the legion or the sign of the eagle, which was an important symbol in ancient Rome. It would not have been decorated with flowers!

7. Lightsaber. The ancient Romans loved to be entertained. Many thousands of people would gather to watch bloody combat sports in huge arenas, such as Rome's great amphitheatre, the Colosseum. All over the empire, slaves and prisoners of war were trained to fight as gladiators – fighting to the death against each other using all sorts of weapons, including weighted nets, swords, spears and harpoons. They never had lightsabers, though – perhaps if they had, more of the gladiators would have survived!

8. Mammoth. The gladiators were also forced to fight many different wild animals, from

bears and lions to rhinos and crocodiles. But they never had to pit their wits against a giant woolly mammoth – they had already been extinct for a thousand years by the time the Romans came along.

9. Electronic scoreboard. The crowd would often judge the performance of a gladiator by

public baths where people went to socialise as well as to get clean. But you wouldn't have found anyone floating around in a rubber ring in those days...

12. Tower block. Around the forum were lots of streets of housing, where poorer Romans rented apartments built in multi-storey blocks. Although they didn't build proper tower blocks like this one, the apartment blocks of ancient

What's afoot in ancient Rome?

making a hand gesture rather than by a score being kept on a scoreboard. It's possible that thumb's down meant 'instant death' but some gladiators occasionally survived to win their freedom.

10. Unicorn. Chariot racing was another popular sport for the ancient Romans but they would not have been pulled along by a unicorn!

11. Rubber ring. Most Roman cities had large

Rome often had several floors. The rooms got smaller and cheaper as you went up and very few had their own water supply or kitchen.

13. Ziggurat. The Romans were the first people to build great domes on their buildings (which is a really difficult thing to do when you don't have machines to help you). They did not build stepped pyramids like this 'ziggurat' – an ancient kind of temple built in Mesopotamia 3,000 years earlier.

14. Cannon. The Roman army had all kinds of helpful machines to help them win their battles. Although they wouldn't have had this cannon, they did have a primitive machine called an 'onager', which worked like a giant catapult to fling great lumps of rock at their enemies.

15. Globe. The Romans drew maps of their enormous empire but there were still huge areas of the world that they didn't know about, like Australia or the Americas. They certainly hadn't worked out that the Earth was a round ball spinning through space, so they would not have had a globe like this one.

16. Trainers. The Romans were very keen on sandals, which were made of leather with straps that often laced part-way up the leg. Roman soldiers put metal studs in the bottom of theirs to help them last better through all the marching, but no one would have had cool trainers like these.

17. Crown. The Romans liked to wear wreaths on their heads to show their importance. They were bestowed as rewards for all sorts of things: bravery, service to the emperor, victory in battle or to celebrate special occasions. There were lots of different types – some made of gold and others made of olive or oak leaves, or even bits of grass. They wouldn't have worn this elaborate coronation crown, though, which is more similar to those later worn by the British monarchy.

18. Geometric print. One popular piece of clothing in ancient Rome was the 'toga' – a long piece of cloth usually woven from white wool, which was draped round the body and worn over a tunic. Different colours of toga were used for different things but only very important people – usually emperors – were allowed to wear purple ones. And no one would have been seen wearing this geometric-print version!

19/20. Ketchup/ pizza. The ancient Romans loved a good feast. The rich liked to show off by having elaborate dinners full of food that was very expensive or difficult to make, rather than caring about whether it tasted any good. One such meal involved stuffing a chicken inside a duck, then inside a goose and inside a pig... and finally stuffed inside a cow! But they would not have covered it all with tomato ketchup. And, although they might have eaten a whole plate of peacock's tongues, they wouldn't have followed it up with a slice of pizza.

5

LIFE IN ANCIENT ROME

The Roman Empire in its heyday stretched over most of the known world, from Britain to North Africa, Spain to Palestine. At its centre was the great city of Rome, and at the centre of the city was the 'forum' – a market square surrounded by temples, baths and stadiums. Here, people gathered to trade goods, visit the public buildings or just hang out with their friends.

Over a thousand years ago, a great civilisation grew in the Americas – the empire of the Mayans. A long time before we had discovered such things in the West, the Mayans made the first calendar, tracked the movements of the planets across the heavens, invented a system of writing and built hundreds of cities across the land that now forms Mexico and Guatemala. But can you spot the 20 things that didn't belong in the time of the Mayans?

6

AT THE TEMPLE OF THE SUN

The Mayans had lived in an area known as Mesoamerica (modern day Mexico and Central America) for hundreds of years but between AD 250 and AD 900 their civilisation really flourished. They built wonderful cities with palaces, stepped pyramids and temples, and they were efficient farmers and brilliant scholars. The problem was that they were also very fond of fighting – their cities were constantly at war with each other and they spent a lot of time capturing prisoners to sacrifice to their gods. By AD 1000, their civilisation had all but disappeared, with their great cities swallowed up by the surrounding rainforests.

I'd rather have a choc ice myself!

1. **Red squirrels** would not have been known to the Mayans as they come from a much colder climate. The rainforests that surrounded their cities were filled with lots of other animals, though – monkeys, jaguars and all manner of exotic birds. The Mayans were excellent hunters and used many of the rainforest animals as a source of food and to make clothing.

2. **Algebraic equation.** The Mayans wouldn't have carved this equation into the wall of their temple, but they did have a sophisticated number system of their own. It used bars and dots instead of the figures 0 to 9. A dot meant 1, a bar meant 5 and the number zero was represented with a symbol that looked like a shell.

3. **Totem pole.** This totem pole was made by the Native Americans of the Northwest Coast rather than by the Mayans, but they did make all sorts of carved objects out of wood, stone, jade and bone.

4. **Pirate.** You wouldn't have seen this 16th-century pirate at a Mayan celebration. But around 500 years after the Mayan civilisation had died out, European invaders arrived in the Americas and conquered the new cultures that had sprung up there – the Aztecs of Mexico and the Incas of Peru. They stole their gold, shipping it back to Europe where – yes, you've guessed – it was often stolen by pirates!

5. **Peacock feather.** Wealthy Mayans loved to wear feathers sewn into cloaks and made into elaborate headdresses. The more important the person, the bigger their hat or headdress. They had lots of beautiful birds' feathers at their disposal: parrots, macaws, hummingbirds and – most importantly – quetzals, which have the longest feathers of any bird. They wouldn't have used the feathers from a peacock, though – they live hundreds of miles away in India.

6. **Pile of presents.** The Mayans had no central king. Instead, each major city had its own ruler and though his subjects would have brought him lots of gifts, they wouldn't have been wrapped up in paper and bows. Apart from beautiful objects carved from jade or jewellery, one of the most useful presents you could give your king was a bunch of prisoners captured from a neighbouring city, either to be used as slaves or sacrificed at the temple to appease the gods.

7. **Watch.** The Mayans loved to wear elaborate jewellery, but this didn't extend to wearing wristwatches, which weren't invented until the 1860s. Although they didn't have any kind of clock, they did use their knowledge of astronomy and mathematics to devise calendars. One was a solar calendar like ours, based on 365 days in a year. The other had a year of 260 days and was used for religious ceremonies. You can see a solar calendar carved into the wall behind the king.

and were skilled dental surgeons. And while we're on the subject of teeth, one popular thing amongst wealthy Mayans was to have holes carved in their teeth that were filled with precious stones like jade or turquoise... Ouch!

10. Stripy socks. The Mayans wove beautiful

would press their children's heads between two wooden boards to flatten them out!

12. Doll. Though they wouldn't have had a plastic doll like this one, the Mayans did make toys for their children, like the wheel-along jaguar you can see in the picture. One strange fact about Mayan society is that,

version was flavoured with chilli and other spices. You can see a cocoa pod in the picture – the beans were considered so valuable that they were sometimes used as money.

15. Elephant. Although the Mayan kings would not have had this Indian elephant to carry them about, they did have an alternative. Their every need was provided for by their subjects and this extended to them being carried from place to place in 'litters' (a kind of chair suspended on long poles) by their slaves.

Did you spot 20 Mayan mistakes?

16. Telescope. The Mayans were excellent astronomers and they kept detailed records of the movement of the stars, Sun, Moon and the planets, but they would not have had this telescope to help them.

17. Map of the Solar System. Nor would they have had the advantage of this modern map of the planets. In fact, they didn't think of them as planets at all – they thought that the stars, Moon and Sun were all gods moving about in the heavens. So no wonder they watched their movements so closely.

18. Basketball game. Every Mayan city had a ball court where the game of 'ulama' was played. Although it was a bit like modern basketball, the players had to compete against each other to get a large ball through a stone ring on the side of the pitch, rather than a net – and they had to do it using only their knees, elbows or hips!

8. Crucifix. The Mayans were very religious people but they did not worship a Christian god and would not have worn a crucifix. They had lots of different gods who could change themselves into different shapes.

9. Plaster cast and crutch. Although they didn't have hospitals, the Mayans were pretty skilled at medicine. Shamans or 'medicine men' were very important people in Mayan society and though they couldn't have put your leg in plaster, they did stitch wounds using human hair; set fractures using wooden splints

fabric out of cotton, often dyed bright colours. However, nobody would have been seen wearing these stripy socks since there were no sheep for them to get the wool from!

11. Spectacles. The Mayans did not have spectacles to improve their eyesight, but they did try to alter their eyes in other ways. It might seem peculiar to us, but the Mayans thought that having crossed eyes was a sign of great beauty, so they would dangle a bead on a string between a newborn baby's eyes until they were permanently crossed. They thought flat foreheads were pretty attractive, too, and

although they put wheels on toys like this, they didn't have any wheeled vehicles themselves!

13. Maharajah. You wouldn't have found the Mayan kings dressed up like this Indian maharajah but they did wear a kind of turban – a long piece of cloth wrapped around their heads and then decorated with feathers, seashells and precious stones.

14. Ice cream cone. Many foods enjoyed in the world today were first cultivated in ancient America but ice cream wasn't one of them! However, they did have cocoa beans and used them to make a drink a bit like the hot chocolate we drink today, except that their

19. Spaceship and alien. The Mayans developed a complex writing system of around 700 symbols called 'glyphs'. They were carved on stone tablets, on the walls of temples and also written in books called 'codices' – made of bark, cloth or animals skins and folded like a concertina. But though they were the first Americans to develop pictorial writing, they would not have used a symbol depicting a spaceship or an alien head!

20. Buddha. The Mayans had a number of gods but Buddha was not one of them. The most important god was the Sun god and they believed that he would not continue his journey across the sky if they did not make sacrifices to him.

1. Mermaid. All Viking ships were built from overlapping planks of wood and had a matching prow and stern, often carved in the shape of a dragon or snake to frighten their enemies. They would not have had a figurehead in the shape of a mermaid (that wouldn't have frightened anyone)!

2. Pirate flag. Although the word 'viking' probably means 'pirate' and they did go around fighting and plundering all over the place, they would not have flown a flag showing a skull and crossbones. Instead, they often flew a flag bearing the sign of the raven – a bird associated with Odin, the father of all the gods.

3. Ship's lantern. Vikings carried flaming torches rather than lanterns to light their way, posting them along the coast near settlements as a signal to returning boats.

4. Aeroplane. The Vikings could not have travelled by plane – a form of transport that would not be invented for a thousand years. However, they did travel further than many other people of their age. One famous Viking, a brave explorer called Leif Eriksson, became the first European to land in North America. He named it Vinland (wine land) after the grapes he found growing there.

5. Galleon. Viking longboats were quite different in shape to this galleon – a type of ship that did not appear until the 16th century. They were powered by oars as well as wind and each had a single central sail. The longboats could sail up shallow rivers to raid inland settlements and when they could not sail it any further, the crew would get out and carry their boat, or roll it over logs, until they reached the next river.

6. Ship's wheel. To help control the direction of their boats, Viking sailors used a steering oar positioned at the back of the boat. They did not have a wheel to help them steer... so it's a wonder they managed to get anywhere, really!

7. Chinese man. The Vikings were great traders, bringing back furs, timber, food and cloth, as well as treasure from their travels. In the year AD 793 they raided the monastery of Lindisfarne, off the coast of Northern England, and brought back many of the monks captured there as slaves. However, they wouldn't have captured this Chinese man as the Far East was unknown to them.

8/9. Bowler hat/ bobble hat. As skilled metalworkers, Vikings were brilliant at making armour. Their helmets were made of hammered steel plates riveted together and lined with cloth padding, sometimes with a nose shield for extra protection. Neither of these hats would have been much use against a sword or spear.

10. Buttons. Vikings wore tunics made of linen or leather, which they also wore beneath chain-mail shirts if they were going fighting. But instead of using buttons to fasten their clothing, they used draw strings or beautifully carved brooches made of pewter, silver or gold.

11. Surfboard. Despite being excellent seafarers, Vikings would not have extended this skill to surfboarding!

12. Macaws (a type of parrot from the Amazon rainforest) would not have been known to Vikings, but they may have kept a raven as a pet instead.

13/14. Snakes and ladders game/ dart. When they weren't sailing the high seas, Vikings loved to play all sorts of games. A quick-thinking board game called Hnefatafl tested their strategic skills, and they also carved walrus tusks into beautiful pieces with which to play chess. But they didn't play Snakes and Ladders (they didn't have ladders and they didn't like snakes much, either!), nor would they have played darts.

15. Quill pen and ink pot. The Vikings used a special alphabet of letters called 'runes'. They believed that the god Odin had given them the runes as a gift so they were treated with great respect. They also thought that runes had magic powers and could be used to tell the future. Because they did not have paper, or writing materials like this, they used knives to carve the runes into wood or stone, or painted them onto pieces of horn or bone to carry with them as lucky charms.

16. Hairbrush. Despite their warring ways, Vikings were very clean people. They washed their faces every morning, bathed once a week

What's wrong in the picture?

(which was more than most people in those days) and even carried special spoons with them to clean the dirt out of their ears! Most Vikings wore their hair long – the men as well as the women. To keep it tidy, they made some of the first combs, carved out of bone, so they could comb their hair everyday. But they wouldn't have had hairbrushes.

17. Compass. The Vikings were skilled navigators but they had little in the way of equipment to help them find their way at sea. Instead, they studied the movement of seabirds, whales and other creatures of the ocean, as well as relying on the position of the Sun and stars and the shape of landmasses to help guide them. They also used a sunstone, made from a piece of crystal, to help them find the position of the Sun even when it was foggy. A primitive navigational tool called a 'lodestone', made of a lump of magnetic ore and used with a needle, helped show them the direction of north and south.

18. Flintlock pistol. Most Vikings were skilled at making weapons, but guns like this would not be invented for another 500 years. Instead, they fought mainly with swords and axes, although they also had daggers, spears and bows. Iron swords were their most important weapons.

19. Cotton reel. Viking maidens were expert weavers, making linen and wool for clothing that they sewed together with bone needles and fastened with metal brooches or pins. They did not have cotton or cotton reels.

20. Wine glass. Only the richest Vikings had any form of glassware because it was so difficult to get hold of – and even then it would have been fashioned into thick vessels rather than this fine glass. Instead, they would have drunk beer and wine from hollowed-out horn cups, often carried around their necks on leather straps.

7

SAILING WITH THE VIKINGS

Vikings were the great raiders and traders of medieval Europe. Life in their Scandinavian homeland was pretty harsh so they set sail in search of food, treasure and slaves from other lands. Thanks to their shipbuilding skills, the Vikings were able to travel far and wide across the oceans, reaching the coast of the Americas nearly 500 years before Christopher Columbus managed it. They built settlements in northern Europe, Iceland, Greenland, the Mediterranean and Russia, and even reached the coast of northern Africa.

They built different ships for different jobs – sleek, fast longboats for raiding trips and fatter, slower vessels called 'knarrs' for carrying cargo. Sometimes brave Viking warriors were even buried with their ships (imagine digging that hole) or the ship was set on fire and sent out to sea with the dead warrior and all his possessions on board. The Vikings believed that the ship would sail to Valhalla, a kind of heaven where only warriors could go.

Wow, we were pretty cool!

JOUSTING WITH THE KNIGHTS

The age of knights lasted for 400 years, all through the medieval period (also known as the Middle Ages), when these horseback warriors could be found all over Europe, fighting in battles for their king and country. When they weren't busy fighting, knights kept in practice by performing in jousting tournaments. Everyone would turn out to watch, from the lords and ladies to the village peasants, but there are 20 things that you wouldn't have seen at this jousting match. Can you find them all?

JOUSTING WITH THE KNIGHTS

It was the duty of every medieval knight to learn how to fight for his lord and it took many years of training. Taking part in jousts helped keep both the knight and his horse in tip-top condition, since being a knight involved not just skill with weapons but supreme fitness and strength. Every knight had his own colours and would display these on his banner and the cloths covering his armour and horse.

When the tournament came to town it was a colourful affair – involving mock battles between knights as well as jousting competitions, and lots of feasting, music and dancing.

It's getting pretty hot in here, folks!

1st

1. **Window.** No medieval castle would have had glass windows. During the Middle Ages people had to be prepared for war at any time, so they built castles to protect themselves from their enemies. A great iron gate called a 'portcullis' often guarded the entrance, and the only 'windows' were slits in the stonework high up in the walls, through which archers could fire their arrows.

2. **Motorbike.** There were very few forms of transport in medieval times and certainly no motorbikes, which weren't invented until the 1880s. The rich used carriages or were carried in 'litters' (a covered chair carried on poles), but most people relied on either horses or their own two feet to get around.

3. **Football.** 'Foteball' was a kicking-ball game that had been played in medieval England since the 13th century, but it didn't involve wearing team shirts or even having goal posts. It was played between two teams and had a marked-out pitch, but otherwise it wasn't much like the game we know today. In fact, in those days it was so violent and ruthless that it was often banned!

4. **Tannoy speakers.** People did not use speakers to make announcements in the Middle Ages. Instead town criers or heralds would work their way through the crowds, shouting out any important information so everyone would know what was going on. When a forthcoming joust was first announced, the town crier would shout about it in the streets and the news would spread by word of mouth through the surrounding area. It was always the cause of great excitement and the banners of knights would be hung outside of people's houses to show support for their favourite knight.

5. **Headphones.** No one would have been wearing headphones at a medieval jousting match – they weren't invented until the 20th century. There was lots of other entertainment, though, including acrobats, dancing bears, jugglers and minstrels (medieval musicians).

6. **Fizzy drink.** Every knight had his attendants, who were training to become squires and eventually knights themselves. They were the knight's errand runners and servants. Although they might have served refreshments to his supporters, it would have included beer or wine and sweet pastries – rather than cans of fizzy drink.

7. **Sunglasses.** Medieval ladies would not have used sunglasses to shield their eyes from the sun. Instead, they sometimes had veils attached to their hats.

8. Saxophone. Bands of minstrels provided the musical entertainment of the Middle Ages. They would have played all sorts of musical instruments, including lutes, tambourines, recorders, flutes and even triangles – but not a brass saxophone.

or for tournaments and jousting matches. Everyday riding horses were called 'palfreys', and packhorses were used to pull carts or transport goods and equipment.

11. Union Jack. This design would not have

13. North American teepee. 'Pavilions' were the brightly-coloured, circular tents that were set up around the edges of a tournament. They housed the knights and their servants, including their surgeon, who was there to patch up any

17. Green armour. A medieval knight's armour was extremely expensive to produce and was tailor-made to fit the knight perfectly. It involved a complex array of garments, chain mail and iron plate and had to be strong enough to protect the person inside but light enough to allow quick movements when fighting in battle (or at the joust). During the medieval period, armour became more and more complex until, by the 16th century, knights wore full plate armour that covered their whole bodies and could weigh as much as 25 kilogrammes. However, the armour was made of iron and would never have been painted green... even though the Green Knight was one of the knights in the famous legends of King Arthur.

Did you find 20 medieval mistakes?

Speech bubble: I wonder if they'll have a carrot race, too?

Speech bubble: I've heard of the Green Knight but that looks ridiculous!

18. Rosettes would not have been given out to winning knights at tournaments. Instead, the knight competed to win the purse, or prize money. Can you find a knight being given a bag of money somewhere in the scene? But apart from the cash, fame and glory were two important reasons why knights fought in jousts.

19. Motorbike helmet. A helmet was an essential part of a knight's armour. Early helmets were a bit like metal hats, but as helmet design developed they began to cover the whole face with air holes so that the knight could breath and eye slits so he could see (though not very well). Some helmets also had conical tops that could deflect blows more easily. It wasn't until the early 14th century that helmets with moveable visors were invented, and they certainly didn't look anything like this modern motorcycle helmet

9. Camel. No knight would have been seen riding a camel, but his horses were among his most prized possessions. War horses were more expensive than normal riding horses and a special kind of war horse, called a 'destrier', was famous for its abilities in battle and was the most desired horse of all.

10. Horsebox. A knight would not have moved his horses around in a horsebox, even though he would have had quite a few of them. Knights had three different kinds of horse, named after their uses rather than their breed. 'Chargers' (or war horses) were used for riding into battle

featured as a knight's colours in medieval times, since it was not created until 1801. It combines the three flags of England, Wales and Ireland into the national flag of Great Britain. Special knights called 'crusaders' fought under the red cross of St George. Can you find one in the picture?

12. Dalmatian dog. Dogs were an important part of medieval life. Kings and nobles often had packs of hounds that they used to hunt deer, wild boar and even bears and wolves. Farmers used them to catch rats and other vermin. However, Dalmatians originally came from the Dalmatia region of Eastern Europe and were not developed as a breed until the 19th century.

wounds. They wouldn't have had a tent shaped like this teepee.

14. Mayan warrior. Knights would have come from far and wide to compete in a tournament but you wouldn't have found this Mayan warrior from the Americas there.

15. Dragon. There are many myths and legends about brave knights fighting off fearsome, fire-breathing dragons but there were no real dragons in medieval Europe.

16. Vulture. Falconry was a popular sport in the middle ages. A falconer would train hawks and falcons to catch small birds and animals, but he would not have had this Egyptian vulture.

20. Coat of arms with a koala and cockatoo. Tournament crowds could identify their favourite knight by his coat of arms – a personal combination of colours and objects that was used on his shield, surcoat and horse draperies. You might expect to see stags, lions, eagles or dragons but not a koala or a cockatoo from Australia (since no one in Europe even knew they existed). Most coats of arms also featured a motto, usually in Latin. Can you see one that means 'brave in difficulties'?

THE EMPEROR'S PARADE

9

Imagine riding on the back of an elephant all bedecked in velvet and jewels. That's just what the emperor of the great Mughal Empire did in India over 500 years ago. He owned hundreds of elephants that were used to fight in battles or in great parades to show off to his subjects. The Mughals built beautiful palaces, wore colourful costumes embroidered with precious stones, and encouraged the work of poets, artists, architects and musicians. However, there were many things they did not have. Can you spot 20 things that look out of place in this scene?

1. Penny farthings were the first machines to be called 'bicycles' but they weren't invented until the 1880s, so you wouldn't have found a painting of one hanging on a Mughal emperor's wall. To get around their empire, Mughals would have walked or ridden on horses, camels or elephants!

2. Cubist painting. This style of painting did not become popular until the early 20th century, when painters like Pablo Picasso started to experiment with new painting styles. In the time of the Mughals, 'miniatures' were the most popular form of painting – small, incredibly detailed pictures painted on cloth or paper using brilliant colours.

3. Heart locket. This Mughal princess would not have had a locket in the shape of a heart but she would probably have owned some more impressive jewellery, such as beautifully carved emeralds, rubies, diamonds and strings of beads or pearls (they often wore as many as 15 strings at a time).

4/5. Sheet music/ gramophone. Although humans had been making musical notations since the earliest times – carved into stone tablets by the ancient Greeks or handwritten in medieval manuscripts – printed sheet music like this did not become common until the 19th century. Similarly, gramophones or phonographs were the first record players, invented around the same time for the mechanical reproduction and recording of sound. Despite this, many of the Mughal emperors were devoted to music and had many musicians as part of their court, passing on their music orally rather than by writing it down. Instruments played would have included the 'rudra vina' or 'been' (the most ancient stringed instrument in India), the barrel drum and the 'surmandal' – an instrument of many strings.

6. Stamped, addressed envelopes would not have been a Mughal emperor's way of sending or receiving messages and letters, but he could have used a pigeon instead. Pigeons were important in communications and pigeon-flying was a popular pass-time, where they would be trained to complete complicated manoeuvres in the air. One emperor, Akbar, was said to have

more than 20,000 birds. Can you find a pigeon carrying a message in the picture?

7. Aftershave lotion. Neither the emperor nor his queen would have had a modern bottle of perfume or aftershave, but both would have bathed in rosewater – which is still made in India today and used both as a food flavouring as

well as in perfume. They even rubbed their horses with it so they would smell good. One Mughal princess is also credited with the discovery of rose oil, or 'attar'. The rose petals were also distilled to make rose liqueur for the wealthy to drink – thousands of flowers were needed to make one small bottle!

8. Mermaid tattoo. No emperor would have been seen sporting this mermaid tattoo but the Mughals were responsible for introducing another kind of body art to India from their Persian homeland – the use of 'henna'. This plant dye was used to stain women's fingertips and to paint intricate patterns on the hands and feet, as well as being used to dye fabrics, hair, even men's beards!

9. Zebra pattern. The embroidered design on a Mughal emperor's clothing is unlikely to have included a bunch of stripy African zebras, but the Mughals did make luxurious robes of muslin, silk, velvet and brocade, often embroidered with gold and silver thread. They depicted intricate images of landscapes, flowers and all manner of birds and beasts.

What's wrong in Mughal India?

10. Daffodils were not known in Mughal India but another flower – the rose – held great importance, not just for its perfume but for its medicinal properties. It is said that the first Mughal emperor, Babur, brought camel-loads of Damask roses from Persia with him when he came to rule and all his daughters were named after roses. Almost all the portraits painted in this period show the subject holding a rose in their hands.

11. Umbrella. This gent's umbrella would have been very out of place in Mughal India. There, they would have had beautifully decorated

parasols to use as protection from the heat of the Sun, rather than waterproof umbrellas to keep off the rain.

12. Armoured rhinoceros. Although they would not have had this armoured rhino, the Mughals did use lots of elephants in their battles, to pull cannons or carry guns, or to ride into battle. The most valuable were covered in armour of quilted cloth, or leather covered with chain

mail and steel plates, often adorned with intricate designs. Various kinds of weapons were sometimes fastened to the elephant's trunk, including swords, scythes or maces.

13. Armoured tanks were not used in battle until the 20th century but when it came to fighting, the Mughals weren't short on firepower. In addition to rifles, they had huge cannons, mortars and large mobile guns pulled along by elephants or horses. The 'zamburak' was a swivel gun mounted on the back of a camel. Can you see one in the picture?

14. Steam trains were not introduced to India until the mid-19th century, when they were introduced by the British to help in the transport of troops and goods – especially cotton – back to Britain.

15. The Eiffel Tower would not have graced the skyline of Mughal India. However, one emperor, Sha Jahan, was responsible for the creation of another of the world's most famous buildings – the Taj Mahal. It was created out of white marble as a tomb for his beloved wife and took over 17 years to build.

16/17. Zoo sign/ ostrich. Modern, public zoos did not appear until the late 19th century, but like many ruling families the world over the Mughals kept menageries of exotic animals for their own pleasure, including lions, cheetahs, deer and, of course, elephants. They were also famed for building beautiful formal gardens, with fountains, pools and lots of beds of sweet-smelling roses. And whilst they may have had peacocks wandering around in them, you would have been unlikely to find this ostrich.

18. Tuk-tuks (a three-wheeled vehicle used as a taxi) wouldn't have been used to carry people in the emperor's parade, although they are a common sight on the streets of modern India. Instead, people would ride on the back of elephants in a specially made seat, called a 'howdah', or a covered chair carried on long poles called a 'palanquin'. Can you see both in the picture?

19. Elizabethan lady. Although this Elizabethan lady would not have appeared in a Mughal emperor's parade, one of the first Englishmen to visit India, Ralph Finch, did so during her reign. Partly as a result of his visit, the East India Company was founded in the year 1600 and set off with the Queen's permission to trade in the riches that he had seen there.

20. Tricorne hats would not have been worn by members of the emperor's court. The most common form of headwear at this time was the turban – the most important accessory for any man as it proclaimed his status, religion and origins. To have it forcibly removed was the most humiliating punishment that could be inflicted! Mughal emperors often had elaborate ornaments attached to their turbans, made of gold and precious gems such as rubies, sapphires, emeralds and diamonds.

THE EMPEROR'S PARADE

During the 16th century, a new dynasty – the Mughals – came to rule India. They came originally from Persia and over the next 200 years a series of emperors built a great empire that included almost all of modern-day India. As well as encouraging the arts, they also built one of the world's most famous buildings – the Taj Mahal – and helped spread the religion of Islam across the region. But by the 18th century the empire began to disintegrate and the rule of the Mughals came to an end.

PIRATES AHOY!

Sailing the ocean waves in the 17th and 18th centuries meant keeping a good lookout for pirates, especially if you had precious goods on board. During this golden age of piracy, the robbers of the high seas swooped on defenceless ships using their smaller, faster sailing sloops, stealing their valuable cargo and sometimes sinking the ship to hide their crimes. In those days, the Caribbean was one of the richest hunting grounds for pirates, chasing galleons loaded with treasure from the Americas across the waters. But can you spot 20 things they wouldn't have laid eyes on back then?

10

PIRATES AHOY!

Everyone thinks that pirates were only interested in treasure – jewels, money, gold and the like – but often they were more interested in stealing things like grain (even pirates have to eat!), bales of cloth, weapons or slaves. Some weren't pirates at all – they plundered Spanish ships under orders, taking back the loot to their own king and country in return for reward money. They were called 'privateers'. Others, the 'buccaneers', were the true pirates, using their own ships to spread terror on the high seas.

Squawk! Pieces of eight!

1. Lighthouse. Pirates had to rely on good seamanship to keep them from wrecking their ships on the rocks, not modern lighthouses like this. Another way of looking out for danger was to climb the rigging (the sails, masts and ropes) to get a better view but this was dangerous work for even the most skilled crewmen.

2. Metal detector. If a pirate buried his treasure to hide it, he would not have had a metal detector to help him find it again. Instead, he would have had to rely on his memory or a well-drawn map. Captain Kidd was one famous privateer who allegedly buried his treasure on an island off the coast of America. He never returned to dig it up – before he had the chance, he was arrested, charged with piracy and hanged.

3. Sou'wester. No buccaneer would have been seen wearing this natty sou'wester, even though it would have kept him nice and dry in a rainstorm. Instead, pirates wore clothing seized from captured prisoners, so they often had flamboyant outfits: doublets (a type of jacket) and waistcoats decorated with ornate braids and made from richly coloured materials, such as velvet or brocade, all topped off with a leather tricorne (three-pointed hat).

4. Sandcastle. Pirates were too busy looting and plundering to spend time building sandcastles but they did build themselves wooden huts for shelter. They were sometimes surrounded by a stockade (a high fence of wooden posts) to keep out anyone trying to steal their treasure.

5/6. Cruise liner/ submarine. Ships like this did not appear until modern times. Instead, many pirates favoured a type of ship called a 'sloop'. With its many sails and shallow draft (the bit between the waterline and the bottom of the boat) it was fast, easy to manoeuvre and could enter inlets and bays where the water was not deep enough for larger ships to follow. Handy if you're trying to escape!

7. Sea monster. Although there are many myths and legends about deep-sea monsters attacking ships, there's no evidence to show that it ever really happened. However, the site of an enormous whale breeching must have been a frightening enough prospect for even the most hardened seafarer and may have given rise to such tales.

8. Duck. Pirates are often portrayed carrying parrots on their shoulders but never ducks. One reason for this comes from a famous novel called *Treasure Island*, a story all about pirates, written by Robert Louis Stevenson in 1881. One of the main characters is a villainous pirate called Long John Silver, who has a wooden leg and carries a parrot on his shoulder. The book was so successful that it influenced how people think of pirates ever since.

to cover an eye injury (and they were pretty common, thanks to all that fighting).

11. Atlas. Pirate captains did not have an atlas to refer to when sailing the oceans but they did have maps and charts to help them navigate their way. These were highly prized drawings,

13. TV aerial. No pirate hut would have come with satellite TV for entertainment. If they were ashore for long periods (hiding out or waiting for the right sailing conditions), pirates had to provide their own entertainment, spending their time drinking, playing music and singing sea-shanties.

could last for up to 12 months if kept dry (though they tasted pretty horrid even when they were fresh!). Without proper food, and especially fresh fruit and vegetables, many pirates got sick and died of a disease called 'scurvy'.

16. Helicopter symbol. You would not have found a symbol of a helicopter on this Spanish 'doubloon' (a type of coin), since they were not invented until the 1900s.

17. Binoculars would not appear for another hundred years. Instead, pirates would have used a telescope, or spyglass, to scan the distant horizons, looking for land or ships to attack. They would also have used a compass to find North, and a backstaff to measure the height of the Sun in the sky at midday, thereby calculating latitude.

18. Map of Australia. Even though pirates sailed far and wide across the oceans, they never made it as far as Australia. One popular place for pirates to hide out was the many islands that make up the Caribbean. For over 200 years this region was a haven for pirates of all kinds until, in the 1700s, better-equipped navies restored order to the high seas and the golden age of pirates came to an end.

19. Matches like this were not invented until the 1800s. Up until then, lighting a fire was a pretty laborious business. To create a flame, first you had to produce sparks by striking a piece of flint against a steel rod and using it to catch alight a piece of cloth, rotten wood or other flammable material. Once this material, (the 'tinder') was alight, they would blow on it to produce a flame. Then they would use it to light their fire.

20. Passports did not come into common use until the 20th century but some privateers did carry other important documents to help identify them. These were called Letters of Marque and were licences issued by a government to authorise the privateer to attack and capture enemy ships.

Did you find 20 pirate problems?

9. Life jacket. If you fell overboard on a pirate ship you wouldn't have had a life jacket to help you keep afloat. The best you could hope for was to be thrown a rope or to be close enough to land to swim ashore.

10. Monocles (a type of eye glass) were not invented until the 1800s, but pirates are often shown wearing eye patches. Like the parrot and the wooden leg, this is largely down to stories written about pirates rather than the truth. However, pirates would have worn a patch

showing land formations as well as shallows, rocks and other features. They were a key part of any pirate's navigational equipment, along with a compass to find North and a backstaff (a measuring device) to calculate their position in relation to the Equator. Can you see someone using a backstaff in the picture?

12. 'I Love Treasure' badge. No pirate would have worn a badge like this. But they were fond of wearing jewellery (usually from the spoils of their latest plunder), including earrings, rings, pins, brooches and pendants, as well as fancy buckles on their shoes.

14. Hamburger. The pirate diet would not have included hamburgers and chips (or ketchup, for that matter). When ashore, pirates would have shot game or caught fish and cooked them on open fires. They would have loaded the ship with as many provisions as possible, including salted meat (which kept for longer) and some live chickens for eggs. But after just a few weeks, most of the fresh food would either have rotted or been eaten!

15. Tinned food would have been very useful on long voyages but unfortunately the canning of food wasn't invented until the 1800s. Instead, pirates had to rely on salted meat, dried beans and (most importantly) hardtack – biscuits that

DID YOU SPOT
THE MISTAKES?